PARTY PLANNING PROJECTS

FOR A LAZY CRAFTERNOON

By STELLA FIELDS

CAPSTONE PRESS
a capstone imprint

Lazy Crafternoon and Snap are published by
Capstone Press
A Capstone imprint
1710 Roe Crest Drive
North Mankato, Minnesota 56003
www.mycapstone.com

Library of Congress Cataloging-in-Publication Data is available on the
Library of Congress website.

ISBN: 978-1-5157-1437-8

Summary: Use this craft book to spend a lazy crafternoon making
party and decorating projects with your friends.

Designer: Lori Bye
Creative Director: Heather Kindseth
Photos: Karon Dubke/Capstone Studio

Projects crafted by Lori Blackwell, Mari Bolte, Lori Bye,
Sarah Holden, Heather Kindseth, Marcy Morin, Sarah Schuette

Image credits: Shutterstock: Africa Studio, 5 (bottom right), Ann Haritonenko, back cover (right), 5 (middle),
Kaponia Aliaksei, back cover (left), MANDY GODBEHEAR, 5 (top), wavebreakmedia, 5 (bottom left)

Design Elements: Shutterstock: luanateutzi, pixelliebe, Studio Lulu, Tossaporn Sakkabanchom

Special thanks to Dede Barton, Shelly Lyons, and Mari Bolte

Printed and bound in the USA.
009687F16

CONTENTS

LAZY CRAFTERNOON   4

SUPPLIES   7

RIBBON CHANDELIER   8

FABRIC BUNTING   10

DECOUPAGE MASON JAR   12

DIY TASSEL GARLAND   14

PAPER DECOUPAGE LETTERS   17

HANGING FLOWER BALLS   18

CONFETTI BALLOONS   20

PAPER FLOWER GIFT TOPPERS   22

WASHI GIFT WRAP   24

DIY ENVELOPES   26

SALADS ON A STICK   28

RAINBOW FRUIT IN GLITTER CUPS   30

LAZY CRAFTERNOON

A lazy crafternoon is a day you spend with your friends, each of you making something incredible. Doesn't sound lazy, right? But it can feel like it, especially with the fun, pretty party projects in this book.

These projects can be done on your own — nothing requires more than one person — but it's always more fun to spend a lazy crafternoon making things with your friends. The crafts in this book are great for beginners, but they can be taken to a new level by crafters with more experience. Invite girls who already craft on their own, but don't stop there. Your fashionista friend already has a great sense for fabric. Your musician friend knows how to put things together. Your movie-loving friend has an eye for what looks great.

You'll need plenty of supplies. You can choose projects from this book and stock the supplies yourself, or just ask your friends to bring what they have. Many of the projects here use things you already have around the house.

Before your friends arrive, get everything set up in your crafting space. You can craft on your bedroom floor or outside, but you might want to find a table where you can lay out the supplies and have room for everyone to work.

Snacks on sticks or cut into small, bite-sized pieces are great choices for people who don't want to get their hands dirty mid-craft. Check out page 28 for a perfect snack to serve your friends, and page 30 for a way to make a fruit salad sparkle.

That's it! Now get lazy.

SUPPLIES

acrylic paint
balloon pump
beads
bias tape
cardstock
clear jumbo balloons
clear plastic cups
clear tape
colored paper
confetti
cording
craft knife

iron
LED candle
mason jars
needle and thread
paper
paper funnel
paper lantern
paper mache letters
pencil

craft punch
decoupage glue
double-sided tape
embroidery hoop
fabric
gift box
gift tags
glitter
glue
hot glue
hot glue gun

plastic utensils
ribbon
ruler
scissors
scrapbook paper
sewing machine
solid wrapping paper
stapler
tissue paper
twine
washi tape
wire
wooden skewers
yarn

RIBBON CHANDELIER

Every room needs a chandelier. Bring color and surprise to your decor with this simple project.

WHAT YOU'LL NEED

14 inch (35.5 cm) embroidery hoop
variety of ribbons in different
widths and textures

3

These imperfect knots add to
the fun of the chandelier!

1 Cut ribbon to varying lengths, between 18-24 inches
(46-60 cm) long. Tie each piece to the embroidery hoop.

2 Keep adding and trimming until the chandelier feels
complete. Make sure to mix up your materials so the
colors, textures, and designs are spread out.

3 Tie three 18-inch- (46-cm) long pieces of ribbon to the
hoop at equal distances around the circle. Knot them
together, and hang from a hook.

Want more detail? Add pom-poms, bells, shells,
and lace. After being used to decorate a party, this
chandelier will look amazing in your room!

Nothing says "party time" like bunting! Hang this easy party banner around the room for an instant crafternoon feel. Fabric, sewing supplies, and bias tape are all you need to bring everything together.

FABRIC BUNTING

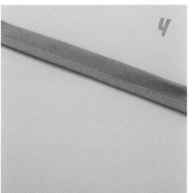

1 Use a piece of cardstock and a ruler to make a triangle template. The triangle should be about 6.5 inches (16.5 cm) wide and 8.5 inches (21.5 cm) tall.

2 Trace the template onto the fabric and cut out the triangles. You'll need two triangles for each piece.

3 Stack each pair of triangle pieces with their right sides together and sew (or glue) along the long edges. Trim any stray threads, turn the triangles right side out, and iron them flat.

4 Sew (or glue) the first 6 to 8 inches (15 to 20 cm) of bias tape shut. Then open the tape and tuck the short end of a triangle between the folds. Sew (or glue) the bias tape shut, sandwiching the triangle inside. Continue adding triangles and sewing or gluing.

5 Once all the triangles are used up, sew (or glue) a 6- to 8-inch (15 to 20 cm) tail at the end of the bias tape. Your banner is now ready to hang!

You can use just a few different fabrics for a streamlined look, or choose dozens to use up leftovers and make a multi-colored bunting. Either way, it'll be gorgeous!

Bring some light to the dark with these delightful luminaries!

DECOUPAGE MASON JAR

WHAT YOU'LL NEED

tissue paper
scissors or circle punch
mason jars
decoupage glue and brush
ribbon or yarn
wire
beads
LED candle

1 Cut the tissue paper into wide strips or use a circle punch to punch out circles of tissue paper.

2 Brush decoupage onto the jar and press tissue paper down, making sure to eliminate any air bubbles. When the jar is covered, add a final coat of decoupage.

3 Glue ribbon or yarn to the top of jar.

4 If you like, add a wire handle by winding wire a few times around the top and making a large loop around the opening. Add beads for a finishing touch.

5 Place LED candles inside jars to illuminate.

These are gorgeous in sunlight, but they're even prettier at night, all lit up by the candles inside. Try different colors of tissue paper to create different illuminated effects.

The perfect party decoration, the tassel garland packs a ton of punch—and all you need is tissue paper!

DIY TASSEL GARLAND

WHAT YOU'LL NEED

tissue paper
scissors
cording, twine, yarn, or other rope
hot glue and hot glue gun

1 Take one piece of tissue paper. Lay it flat, and then fold it in half widthwise. Fold in half lengthwise. Then fold again, lengthwise.

2 Place with the folded edge at the top. Make cuts 0.25 inch (0.6 cm) apart from the bottom up, leaving about 1.5 inches (4 cm) at the top.

3 Unfold, and lay flat so that the fringe is horizontal. Untangle the fringe as necessary.

4 Starting at the bottom, roll up the paper. Once the entire sheet is rolled up, twist the center, tightly and gently.

5 Fold the two sides of tassel slices together. Twist the center around itself, creating a small loop in the top for a string.

6 Add a dot of hot glue to the loop to keep the tassel from untwisting.

Want a decoration in your room that you can change whenever you want? Buy a few different colors of tissue paper, and switch them out when you're bored.

Decorate these letters
for any occasion.

PAPER DECOUPAGE LETTERS

WHAT YOU'LL NEED

paper mache letters
acrylic paint and paintbrush
scrapbook paper in several colors
   and patterns
craft knife
decoupage

1. Paint the sides of the letters with acrylic paint.

2. Flip the letters backward and trace onto scrapbook paper.

3. Using the craft knife, cut out the scrapbook letters.

4. Coat the letter with decoupage. Place the scrapbook paper on top of the cardboard letter, pressing out any air bubbles. Let it dry for a few minutes.

5. While the decoupage dries, cut out any additional shapes you want to add. Layer additional paper with decoupage.

6. When you're done, add another layer of decoupage to the top of the letters to seal the paper.

Spell out a birthday girl's name, or supply each guest's initial and let them decoupage it themselves.

You can use any paper to decoupage these letters — try comic book pages, pages from an old dictionary or book, etc.

Even your living room can feel like a summer garden with these pretty floral puffs.

HANGING FLOWER BALLS

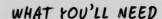

WHAT YOU'LL NEED

scalloped circle craft punch
tissue paper
ribbon
stapler
paper lantern
glue
ribbon

1

2

1 Using a craft punch, cut scalloped circles from tissue paper. You'll need a lot of circles, so plan on punching them out for a while.

2 Stack 8 circles on top of each other. Staple the center of the circles.

3 Fluff the stapled tissue paper up to look like a flower.

4 Glue flowers to the paper lantern. Continue until lantern is completely covered.

5 Hang with a length of ribbon.

3

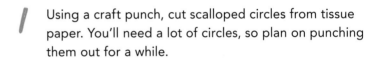
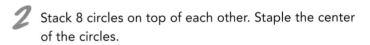
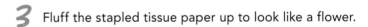

This is the perfect type of project to do while talking to your friends. It's pretty lazy, so your attention can be on your conversation, not so much on what your hands are doing. If you're alone, you could do this while watching a movie.

4

These balloons are extra special!

CONFETTI BALLOONS

Add tissue paper tassels, made using the technique on page 14, for an even prettier decoration.

WHAT YOU'LL NEED

clear jumbo balloons
tissue paper
craft punch
balloon pump
paper funnel

1 Use the craft punch to make confetti out of tissue paper.

2 Fill the balloon with tissue paper confetti. A paper funnel can help make filling the balloon easier.

3 Blow up the balloon and tie to close.

21

Could anything be lovelier than these gorgeous gift decorations?

PAPER FLOWER GIFT TOPPERS

1

WHAT YOU'LL NEED

colored paper or cardstock
scissors
hot glue and hot glue gun

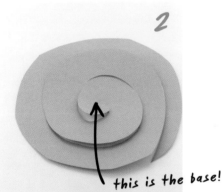

2

this is the base!

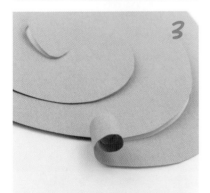

3

5

1 Cut a 6-inch (15-cm) circle from a piece of paper.

2 Cut a spiral in your circle, starting from the outside edge working your way to the middle. As you approach the center of the circle, leave a larger middle area so there is a base. This will be used later for gluing the flower together.

3 Start rolling up the spiral from the outside all the way to the center. Keep it as tight as you can.

4 After rolling up about 1 or 2 inches (2.5-5 cm) of the spiral, add a small dot of hot glue to make sure it still has a nice tight center when you are finished.

5 Stand your tightly coiled spiral upright, using the center piece as a base for your flower, and then let it unravel a little. Add some hot glue to the base and gently lower the rolled flower petals onto the base. Hold until dry.

These make great gift toppers, but see what else you can use them for!

23

Your presents will be so pretty, no one will want to open them!

WASHI GIFT WRAP

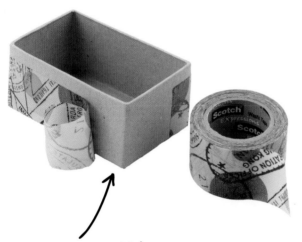

Wrap your gift box in thicker washi tape for a different look!

1 Box your gift in a solid-color gift box. You can use a solid-color wrapping paper if your box has marks on it.

2 Wrap long strips of washi tape all the way around your box.

3 Add tags, ribbon, and twine.

You can't go wrong with this project. If you're wrapping a lot of gifts, do it in stages — wrap all of them first, then add washi tape to each package, and finally add the accents. This will keep your presents from looking alike!

DIY
ENVELOPES

1 Start with a square piece of paper with a corner pointing at you. Use a ruler to help you draw a light line between the corners of the paper to form an X. The center of the X is the center of the square. Fold the corners on the right and left into the center of the X.

2 Fold the bottom point so that the tip is about 0.5 inches (1.2 cm) above the center of the X. Press the fold at the bottom down so it's a sharp crease. Add two strips of double-sided tape to hold the bottom flap in place.

3 Fold the top point down so it overlaps the center by 0.5 inches (1.2 cm). If you want to fasten the top flap in place, use double-sided tape or a sticker.

WHAT YOU NEED:

paper or cardstock
pencil
ruler
double-sided tape or glue

These are much easier than they look!

SALADS ON A STICK

Keep your hands clean for crafting by making easy-to-eat salads on sticks. Just slide bite-size vegetables and cheese cubes onto wood skewers.

Try some of these combinations:

Wedge: iceberg lettuce, bacon, and grape tomato drizzled with ranch dressing and bleu cheese crumbles

Greek: grape tomatoes, feta cheese, cucumbers, black olives, and red onions, drizzled with Greek salad dressing

Sweet Strawberry: strawberries, spinach, and mandarin oranges drizzled with poppy seed dressing

Chef: romaine lettuce, hard-boiled eggs, ham, cucumber, and bread cubes, drizzled with your favorite dressing and shredded cheese

Plain skewers are so boring!
Use one of these ideas to dress them up:
* Fold washi or glitter tape over the sticks and trim to make pennant or flag shapes.
* Cut sticky-back craft foam into shapes, such as circles or stars.
Stick two shapes together with the skewer in the middle.
* Tie ribbon or fabric scraps to the sticks.

RAINBOW FRUIT IN GLITTER CUPS

Glitter makes everything great! Dress up plain fruit with glamorous accessories.

UTENSILS

1 Paint the plastic utensil handles with decoupage glue. Dip the wet handles directly into glitter. Tap off excess glitter, and let the glue dry for at least half an hour.

2 Add another layer of decoupage glue, sprinkling on additional glitter in any bare areas. Let the glue dry completely before using.

WHAT YOU'LL NEED

plastic utensils
clear plastic cups
decoupage glue
glitter
fruit
whipped cream
fresh mint

CUPS

1 Paint the bottom third of the cups with decoupage glue. Sprinkle on glitter, with a heavier layer near the bottom and a lighter layer farther up the cup. Tap off excess. Let the glue dry for at least half an hour. Then cover any glittered areas with another layer of decoupage glue.

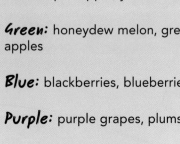

FRUIT

Layer fruits by color for a healthful, rainbowy snack.

Red: strawberries, cherries, watermelon, pomegranate seeds, raspberries, red apples

Orange: oranges, mandarin oranges, mango, cantaloupe, peaches, nectarines, papaya, apricots

Yellow: pineapple, yellow watermelon, bananas, yellow apples

Green: honeydew melon, green grapes, kiwi, pears, green apples

Blue: blackberries, blueberries, currants

Purple: purple grapes, plums, dried cranberries, figs

Serve with a dollop of whipped cream and a sprig of mint.

READ MORE

Bell, Alison. *Let's Party! What's Your Style.* Montreal, Quebec, Canada: Lobster Press, 2005.

Bolte, Mari. *Eco Gifts: Upcycled Gifts You Can Make.* Make It, Gift It. North Mankato, Minn.: Capstone Press, 2015.

Jones, Jen. *Pampering Parties: Planning a Party that Makes Your Friends Say "Ahhh."* Perfect Parties. North Mankato, Minn.: Capstone Press, 2014.

INTERNET SITES

FactHound offers a safe, fun way to find Internet sites related to this book. All of the sites on FactHound have been researched by our staff.

Here's all you do:
Visit www.facthound.com
Type in this code: 9781515714378

LOOK FOR ALL THE BOOKS IN THE SERIES